BÉABA®

YOUR BABY'S FIRST
FOOD
WITH BABYCOOK®

By professional chefs
Christophe Saintagne & **Laura Portelli**
with **Laurence Haurat**, psychologist and nutritionist

80 EASY,
AND CREATIVE
RECIPES

FOR BABIES
FROM 4 TO
24 MONTHS

DUCASSE
EDITION

EDITO

When Christophe Saintagne—chef at the Papillon restaurant in Paris—and his wife, Laura Portelli—chef at Garde-Manger in the 17th arrondissement—met up with psychologist and nutritionist Laurence Haurat, it was to talk about their book: this book on baby nutrition that all three of them wrote with Béaba®.

Together, they wanted to offer parents a book for them to feel confident, sure that their baby's taste buds would be awakened thanks to the creativity of the chefs, doing so safely as a result of Laurence's input, and all hand in hand with Babycook®.

Throughout their conversation, they shared their desires, common values, and their belief in the importance of nutrition in the development of babies as well as families.

Laurence Haurat — Christophe, you've written many cookbooks, what made you write one devoted to babies?

Christophe Saintagne — Émile, our one-year-old baby. Laura and I wanted to share our experience with other parents and suggest recipes that were different from the usual ones, offering more creative ideas. We wanted to get Émile to try everything quickly, but obviously what we did with our baby might not work for all children. That's why we needed your help.

LH — I imagine that you observed your baby with great interest but, above all, that you are both comfortable around nutrition. You know a lot about food. If particular ones are accepted over others when you begin introducing solids, it's because a baby is not a little adult. A young baby's kidneys and digestive tract are not yet mature and some foods can be too aggressive for them if they are given to early, especially if they contain fiber, which is an irritant, or too much salt.

Laura Portelli — It's true that the pace of introducing solids is now more flexible, but we have always been careful. Our child is really curious about food. I have to say, however, that from when he was born, he has always been with us in the kitchen. He sees people eating all day long. He is attracted to what is on our plates, and he wants to try it. He quickly went from purees to more solid food.

LH — That's where you can see to what extent parents' habits and their relationship with food shape a child, even if he or she has their own personality. Yours is an interesting case, but other babies, conversely, need more time. They need to try things a little at a time, and you need to accept that they sometimes refuse what you give them. A child is not little "us"; you need to let your baby be different.

CS — In this book, we wanted to share our experience with Babycook®, because after I discovered it with Paul, our eldest child, we wanted to use it from the start with Émile.

LH — I love this appliance! It's an all-in-one machine, takes up almost no space, is easy to use, and lets you to do everything without having to use ten saucepans. In addition, it steams food, which is the healthiest way of cooking. I used it for the first time with my son 18 years ago, and I'm still crazy about it.

LP — You can take it anywhere, because it's such a handy size. With Babycook®, all you need is water to be "in place," which is what we say in the restaurant business when everything is ready to be cooked. And, after you've taken care to choose good ingredients, it's important to treat them well. We really like steaming, because it is gentle to food and not aggressive to them.

LH — There's something for everyone in this book, because you suggest a lot of flavor combinations. You can imagine how babies' taste buds will open up. When they are young, things are easier, but later on that's not always the case.

CS — That's true, it changes depending on their age. With Paul, our eldest, I noticed that when he was about three or four he would take a "I don't like it" stance. It could have been to be like his classmates, because it coincided with when he started school and ate in the cafeteria.

LH — It's a particular period that's called food neophobia: the fear of trying new things. When they are little, often babies open their mouths wide and eat a little of everything. And then, from about the age of two or three, they close the hatch. It's much more difficult. How did you cope with that moment?

CS & LP — We set boundaries: We didn't make him eat anything he didn't want to, but we didn't replace it. Early on, we said to him, "Mealtimes are very important. If you don't want to eat anything, you'll have to wait until the next one, but you won't get anything in between." It's important to set these limits, and also in regard to behaving at the table as well as not accepting any food demands your child might have. Family mealtimes must be respected.

LH — I agree completely: Setting food boundaries is part of a child's education. The table is a place where, from an early age, you can learn a lot about the ideas your baby has, give him or her the words to express feelings, and teach your child to understand him or herself, to recognize hunger, feeling full, etc.

CS — The table is the perfect place for conveying human values. My aim is for them to be understood and to be lifelong. In involves caring about others, realizing that growing and producing food is no simple matter, transforming it, conveying ideas, giving love.

LH — Actually, it's funny, we talk about educating our children, but they also—in a way—educate us by changing the way we look at food, by making us examine ourselves.

CS — I'd go even farther and say that the whole family can be reeducated. All the recipes in the book are suitable for the entire family. What's good for your baby is good for us, although it's not at all the true the other way around. And then, there is the global act of eating that lets us be aware of the place and responsibility we have in, and for, the environment.

LH — Seeing the recipes that you suggest in the book, I get the feeling that seasonality is extremely important.

LP — Following the rhythm of the seasons lets you play with colors on the plate, and these are different all year round. You don't have the same desires, the same needs, or the same ways of cooking throughout the year. Moreover, by following the seasons, you support farming that is natural and sustainable, and that is essential to be sure that the produce you give to your child is of the best quality.

LH — It's amazing how Nature responds to our needs, with fruit and vegetables that are full of water in summer and produce that requires being cooked at low temperature or for a long time in winter, warming the kitchen as it cooks.

CS — I like raw food myself, especially spring and summer produce that is tender and contains a lot of water. And citrus fruit in winter that has a lot of vitamin C when we need to fight off viruses. This seasonality of produce makes you feel different emotions—tasting the first strawberries in spring is a happy moment.

LH — Yes, that's what fascinating about food, the range of emotions it makes you feel. The way a smell can be linked to a memory, a flavor with a heartwarming situation. Even a dislike for a food can often be shaped by a negative emotion experienced by eating certain produce or a certain dish. At the end of the day, everyone is a special, singular eater with his or her own story, and that's why it's so important to give your baby a solid foundation.

BÉABA®,
BABYCOOK®
AND ITS ACCESSORIES

For 30 years, Béaba® has revolutionized parents' lives with well-designed, innovative, and user-friendly products that simplify their day-to-day lives.

Babycook® steams, blends foods, heats, and defrosts jars of baby food and rapidly becomes an indispensable ally of young parents when it comes to preparing their baby's healthy meals quickly and easily.

In addition, the expanded range has several models of Babycook® to meet the diverse needs parents may have, and it includes ingenious accessories, such as the Rice Cooker, which cooks starchy ingredients, and a wide range of plastic, glass, and silicone storage containers.

P 14
GO GENTLY:
INTRODUCING SOLIDS
IN SMALL STEPS

08

INTRODUCING
FOODS CHART

16

SPRING

P 18
AWARENESS OF
FLAVORS
AND TEXTURES

P 50
QUALITY, THE BEST
FOR MY BABY

SUMMER

48

100

FALL

P 102
THE SENSES:
ALL STIMULATED
BY FOOD

150

WINTER

P 152
BETWEEN ANXIETY AND
DISCOVERY: THE DIFFICULT
JOB PARENTS HAVE
IN NOURISHING
THEIR CHILD

INDEX BY SEASON,
BY PRODUCT
AND BY AGE!

APPENDICES

194

INTRODUCING FOODS CHART

The chart here indicates the different ages for introducing specific foods to your baby to guide you step by step in introducing foods to your baby.

	4 TO 6 MONTHS	7 TO 8 MONTHS	9 TO 12 MONTHS	FROM 13 MONTHS	FROM 18 MONTHS
Artichoke			X		
Arugula (rocket)			X		
Asparagus				X	
Avocado				X	
Baby fava beans (baby broad beans)				X	
Broccoli	X (FLORET)				
Butternut squash	X				
Carrots	X				
Cauliflower			X		
Celeriac		X (COOKED)			
Celery					
Cucumber		X (SEEDED)		X (WHOLE)	
Eggplant (aubergine)			X		
Endive		X			
Fennel	X				
Green beans	X (EXTRA-SMALL)				

VEGETABLES

08

VEGETABLES

	4 to 6 months	7 to 8 months	9 to 12 months	from 13 months	from 18 months
Green bell pepper			X (PEELED)	X (UNPEELED)	
Kale					
Leek	X (WHITE PART)			X (WHOLE)	
Legumes	X				
Olives				X	
Oyster mushroom				X	
Parsnip	X				
Porcini				X	
Potato	X				
Pumpkin	X				
Radish				X	
Red beet (beetroot)	X				
Red bell pepper			X (PEELED)	X (UNPEELED)	
Romanesco broccoli				X	
Rutabaga (swede)		X			
Salad greens	X				
Salsify				X	
Sorrel			X		
Spinach		X			
Snow peas (mange tout)				X	
Sweet potato	X				
Swiss chard		X (LEAVES)			
Tomato		X (PEELED/SEEDED)		X (WHOLE)	
Turnip			X		
Watercress		X			
White beet		X			
White mushrooms				X	
Yam	X				
Zucchini (courgette)	X (SEEDED)				

	4 TO 6 MONTHS	7 TO 8 MONTHS	9 TO 12 MONTHS	FROM 13 MONTHS	FROM 18 MONTHS
FRUITS					
Apple	X				
Apricot	X				
Banana	X				
Blackberries		X			
Cherries		X			
Clementine		X			
Figs			X (WITH OTHER FRUIT)	X (WHOLE)	
Kiwifruit			X		
Lemon		X			
Mango		X			
Melon		X			
Orange		X			
Papaya			X		
Peach	X				
Pear	X				
Pineapple		X			
Quince	X				
Raisins	X (COOKED AND COMBINED)				
Raspberries		X			
Rhubarb			X		
Strawberries		X			
Watermelon		X			
NUTS					
Almonds			X (MEAL)		
Coconut			X		
Hazelnuts			X (MEAL)		
Pistachios			X (MEAL)		
Walnuts			X (MEAL)		

	4 to 6 months	7 to 8 months	9 to 12 months	from 13 months	from 18 months
SPICES, HERBS, SEASONINGS					
Cardamom	X				
Cilantro (coriander)	X				
Colombo curry	X				
Cumin	X				
Curry			X		
Dill	X				
Garlic			X		
Ginger		X			
Mint	X				
Onion			X		
Orange flower water		X			
Parsley	X				
Pepper			X		
Ras el hanout	X				
Rosemary	X				
Saffron	X				
Salt				X	
Shallots			X		
Star anise	X				
Tarragon	X				
Vanilla		X			
Verbena		X			
MEAT					
Andouille sausage					X
Beef		X			
Blood sausage					X
Chicken		X (BREAST)			
Duck		X			
Free-range chicken		X			
Smoked bacon					X

	4 to 6 MONTHS	7 to 8 MONTHS	9 to 12 MONTHS	FROM 13 MONTHS	FROM 18 MONTHS
CEREALS AND LEGUMES					
Baby fava beans					X
Chickpeas (garbanzo beans)					X
Corn (sweetcorn)				X	
Cornmeal			X		
Jerusalem artichoke			X		
Macaroni		X			
Millet					X
Peas		X			
Red lentils				X	
Rice		X			
Semolina		X			
Tapioca		X			
FISH					
Haddock		X			
Pollack		X			
Red snapper		X			
Salmon		X			
Tuna (canned)		X			
Whiting		X			
DAIRY PRODUCTS					
Cream cheese		X			
Goat milk cheese		X			
Parmesan cheese			X		
Ricotta cheese		X			

	4 to 6 months	7 to 8 months	9 to 12 months	from 13 months	from 18 months
EGGS					
Yolks (hard boiled)		X			
Whole eggs, hard boiled or well cooked		X			
PRODUCTS CONTAINING SUGAR					
Chestnut honey				X	
Chocolate				X	
Honey				X	
FATS					
Butter		X			
Crème fraîche		X			
Olive oil		X			
Sunflower oil		X			
OTHERS					
Almond milk				X	
Bread		X (CRUST)		X	
Chestnuts				X	
Coconut milk				X	
Miso				X	
Rice milk				X	
Rice paper wrappers	X				
Tahini				X	

All of the recipes in this book are designed for one to three meals, depending on the age and appetite of your baby. After it has cooled, you can store the leftovers in a sealed container in the refrigerator until the next day.

GO GENTLY:
INTRODUCING SOLIDS
IN SMALL STEPS

The introduction of solid foods is a transitional period awaited eagerly by parents, but with some trepidation, too.

Pediatricians believe that the best time to begin introducing new foods is between 4 and 6 months. Overwhelmed by advice given left, right, and center, young parents are often bewildered and afraid they will do something wrong. Put anxiety and worry aside: The way to tackle this transition for your baby—and for you, too — is to take a go-gently approach.

Go gently, because introducing solid foods is done step by step.

From the start of introducing solids, after the fourth month and by the sixth month, mild-tasting foods —and those that are most appropriate for your baby's digestive tract—are introduced. At first, these are vegetables with soft fibers (carrots, zucchini, young green beans, and broccoli) to start your baby getting used to flavors that are a little bitter and acidic. No salt or sugar is added. Pure flavor, diluted in milk. And always in small amounts, to see how they are accepted. In the hours and days after your baby tries a food for the first time, observe how it is received and check that no allergic reaction or intolerance develops (redness, rash, colic, etc.). There's no rush, no obligation, just the pleasure of discovering new things.

Go gently, too, because now is the time to talk to your baby about what he is eating.

Meals should be accompanied by your voice, by memories, by saying the names of the vegetables, of the fruit.

From 4 months, your baby begins to learn, to remember, to experiment. He touches the food, notices the smells, sees the colors. Babycook® emits steam like a little train; you blend the food and a new sound is taken in. And so, your baby discovers that the bottle contains a new flavor, and all of your little one's senses are stimulated.

Each recipe in this book has been designed and conceived as a journey of multiple discoveries. Step by step, the range of foods your baby eats will be expanded.

And still going gently, little by little, your baby's diet of milk—which is high in fat to encourage growth—will be replaced by foods that are high in carbohydrates (sugars). Vegetables at first, then fruit, and, a little later, starches that will help your baby to grow, sleep, and learn well. Milk, nevertheless, will still be an important part of your baby's diet, because it covers many needs.

Introducing solids really is done gently, because until 1 year of age, it mainly serves to awaken your baby's taste buds and provides him or her with the ability to move on to new foods that will, later on, meet any nutritional requirements.

Go gently, because you should always respect your baby's pace, and your own. Observe your baby's attitude and willingness to approach new foods, his or her ability to appreciate new textures, whether he or she can hold a spoon and then a fork. There's no hurry, don't push; let your baby advance toward this new world at his or her own pace—and at yours. You, too, must feel ready to let your baby grow up.

HERE
AT LAST!

SPRING

FRESH,
COLORFUL
RECIPES!

AWARENESS OF FLAVORS AND TEXTURES

Your baby has not waited until the introduction of solids to become aware of flavors. Absolutely not! Taste buds begin developing during the third month of a mother's pregnancy. From that moment onward, a baby begins to perceive the flavors of what their mother eats and therefore starts to develop a personal flavor database.

Next step: birth. In the early days of life, your baby drinks only milk. And, even now, breast milk is full of flavors. In fact, aromatized molecules are transferred from what the mother eats to the milk, then on to the baby. That is how a baby become aware of flavors and how your baby's food preference is shaped.

Between the end of the fourth month and by the sixth month, the taste and sensory adventure continues for everyone, when introducing solids comes into play (see page 14). A great series of discoveries then begins: What is your baby's appetite like? How is your baby progressing with the discovery of flavors, textures, and his or her environment? Is your baby curious or comforted by flavors he or she already knows and can identify? Every little eater is different. It's why we say, "To each his own". And with good reason! Endowed taste buds that are more, or less, sensitive (for example, in regard to bitterness), each child reacts individually to the introduction of a new food. A baby can express surprise at something unknown and refuse a new food without even tasting it, or your baby may happily open his mouth to longingly discover the surrounding world of flavors.

Then, little by little, your baby will begin to get used to different textures; at first (up to about 9 months), solids are limited to the fine, very smooth textures that the Babycook® lets you prepare effortlessly. Next, a baby's ability to chew evolves. You should no longer worry that food will go down the wrong way, and your baby's digestive tract will be more mature.

18

BEFORE STARTING TO
PREPARE CHRISTOPHE'S RECIPES,
MAKE SURE YOUR BABY CAN
DIGEST EACH OF THE INDIVIDUAL FOODS
BELOW FROM WHEN HE OR SHE
IS FOUR MONTHS OLD.

These developments will let you expand the range of mixtures and move on to thicker, more textured purees. And, yet again, each must be at the baby's own pace. There's no need to rush; sooner or later your child will start to eat small pieces of solid food. Sometimes it only takes a few days to become ready to accept a change.

Finally, from one year of age, small pieces of solid food can be introduced, along with a fork. But again, there's no hurry: Your child will adapt, at his or her own pace, to all these new changes. There are no rules, no obligation, no hurry.

Whatever the development of your baby, stimulation is particularly important, and you can do this by offering new things and introducing changes. Don't give up and never get angry or confrontational. Don't describe your baby as difficult, or as "not liking anything." Give your baby time to evolve and don't pigeonhole your little one too quickly. If these changes don't happen today, they will certainly be just around the corner.

VEGETABLES
GREEN BEANS,
BABY CARROTS,
SALAD GREENS.

FRUITS
BANANA,
SPRING PEAR,
APPLE.

PREPARATION TIME
10 MINUTES

COOKING TIME
10 MINUTES

FROM
7 TO 8
MONTHS

SPINACH, HADDOCK

³⁄₈ ounce (10 g) haddock fillet

2 handfuls fresh spinach

1 teaspoon olive oil

Immerse the haddock into a bowl of water for 15 minutes to desalt it.

Meanwhile, remove the stems from the spinach, wash in a generous amount of water, then dry the leaves well. Put the spinach leaves and haddock into the steamer basket and fill the steamer reservoir to level 2. Cook for 10 minutes. Do not discard the cooking liquid.

When cooked, blend the spinach and fish to a fairly thick puree, adding a little of the cooking liquid, if needed.

From 9 months, drain the haddock when cooked and cut into ⅛-inch (3-mm) dice. Serve the spinach in a bowl and top with the diced fish.

PREPARATION TIME
5 MINUTES

COOKING TIME
15 MINUTES

FROM
7 TO 8
MONTHS

SPINACH, EGG AND POTATOES

½ potato

1 handful spinach

1 egg (whole)

1 teaspoon olive oil

Salt (from 12 months)

Peel the potato and cut it into ⅜-inch (1-cm) dice. Remove the stems from the spinach, wash, and squeeze the water from the leaves. Wash the egg's shell. Fill the water reservoir to level 2 and cook the potato and whole egg in the steamer basket for 10 minutes.

When cooked, remove the hard-boiled egg. Do not discard the cooking liquid. Fill the water reservoir again to level 1, add the spinach and cook again for 5 minutes.

Meanwhile, shell the egg and mash one-quarter of it finely with a fork.

When the potato-and-spinach mixture is cooked, blend to a smooth puree, add a little cooking liquid, if necessary.

Serve topped with the mashed egg. Depending on your child's development, you can also blend the quarter egg with the other ingredients.

From 12 months, you can add a pinch of salt while cooking the potato.

GLOBE ARTICHOKE, ARUGULA

3 globe artichokes
1 lemon
1 small bunch arugula
1 teaspoon olive oil
Salt (from 12 months)

Remove the leaves from the artichokes, trim the hearts, remove the chokes, and cut into ⅜-inch (1-cm) dice.

Cut the lemon in half, then juice one half and pour the juice over the artichokes. Cut a slice from the other lemon half.

Remove the stems from the arugula. Wash and dry the leaves.

Fill the water reservoir to level 2 and cook the diced artichokes with the slice of lemon in the steamer basket for 10 minutes.

When cooked, remove the slice of lemon, put the diced artichokes into the blender, add the arugula leaves and juice of the halved lemon, and blend. Drizzle with the olive oil.

For older children, from 12 months, you can add a pinch of salt while cooking the artichokes.

THE NUTRITIONIST'S TIP

To make life easier, use frozen artichokes, cooking them after they have thawed.

PREPARATION TIME
10 MINUTES

COOKING TIME
10 MINUTES

FROM
9 TO 12
MONTHS

POIVRADE ARTICHOKES, LIME

5 poivrade artichokes
1 lime
1 teaspoon olive oil
Salt (from 12 months)

Remove the leaves from the artichokes, cut them in half, and remove the chokes.

Zest the lime, cut away the pith, and cut into thin slices.

Fill the water reservoir to level 2 and cook the diced artichokes with the lime slices for 10 minutes.

When cooked, put everything into the blender and blend, adding the zest and olive oil, to a smooth puree.

From 12 months, you can add a pinch of salt while cooking the artichokes.

CUCUMBER, DILL, AND CREAM CHEESE

½ cucumber

2 tablespoons cream cheese

1 small sprig dill

Peel and seed the cucumber, then cut into ⅜-inch (1-cm) dice. Mix with the cream cheese and dill (washed and squeezed) just until like a soup and serve cool.

For younger babies, from 7 to 8 months, put the cucumber and dill into the steamer basket, fill the water reservoir to level 2, and cook for 10 minutes before blending with the cream cheese.

PREPARATION TIME
5 MINUTES

COOKING TIME
15 MINUTES

FROM
9 TO 12
MONTHS

PARSLEY ROOT, MACARONI

¼ parsley root or parsnip

¾ ounce (20 g) macaroni

Wash and peel the parsley root, then cut it into ⅛-inch (3-mm) dice. Mix the macaroni and parsley-root brunoise, then put them into the pasta/rice cooker.

Fill the water reservoir to level 3 and cook for 15 minutes. Do not discard the cooking liquid.

When cooked, put the macaroni and parsley root into the blender and blend to a smooth puree, adding a little of the cooking liquid, if needed.

PREPARATION TIME
10 MINUTES
RESTING TIME
15 MINUTES

FROM
9 TO 12
MONTHS

BASIL-SCENTED BREAD AND TOMATO SOUP

3 tomatoes
1 scallion
¼ clove garlic
2 basil leaves
1 chunk of day-old bread
1 tablespoon olive oil

Use a vegetable peeler to peel the tomatoes. Cut them in quarters and remove the seeds. Peel the onion and garlic. Remove the germ from the garlic, if there is one.

Put everything into the blender with a glass of water and the basil leaves, then blend to a thin soup.

Cut the chunk of bread into ⅜-inch (1-cm) dice. Put the diced bread into a bowl and pour the tomato soup over it. Let stand for 15 minutes for the bread to swell before serving and drizzle with a little olive oil.

THE CHEF'S TIP

To make it easier to peel the tomatoes, immerse them for a few seconds in a saucepan of boiling water.

MANGO AND BASIL

1 mango
1 sprig basil

Peel the mango and cut up the flesh. Wash and dry the basil leaves.

Put the mango and basil leaves into the blender without adding water and blend to a smooth puree. Serve cool.

For younger babies, from 7 to 8 months, put the mango and basil into the steamer basket, fill the water reservoir to level 2, and cook for 10 minutes before blending.

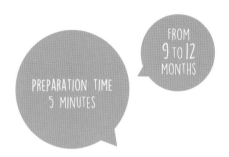

PAPAYA AND CREAM CHEESE SOUP

1 papaya
¼ cup (60 g) cream cheese
1 tablespoon olive oil

Peel and seed the papaya. Coarsely chop and put it into the blender.
Add the cream cheese and blend until smooth.
Serve the soup unheated in a bowl, flavored with a drizzle of olive oil.

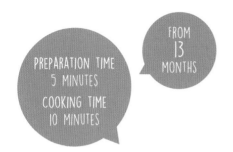

PREPARATION TIME
5 MINUTES
COOKING TIME
10 MINUTES

FROM
13
MONTHS

GREEN ASPARAGUS, TARRAGON

6 asparagus spears

8 tarragon leaves

½ teaspoon lemon juice

1 to 2 teaspoons olive oil

Salt

Wash and peel the asparagus, then remove the hard part of the spears. Cut the asparagus into pieces. Put into the steamer basket, fill the water reservoir to level 2, and cook for 10 minutes with a pinch of salt.

Put into the blender with the tarragon, lemon juice, and olive oil and blend to a smooth soup.

THE CHEF'S TIP

You can sprinkle cooked asparagus tips over the soup to give your baby something to chew.

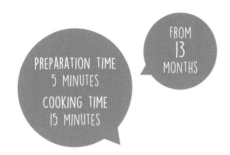

PREPARATION TIME
5 MINUTES
COOKING TIME
15 MINUTES

FROM
13
MONTHS

WHITE MUSHROOMS, HAZELNUTS

5 large white mushrooms

4 teaspoons (10 g) shelled hazelnuts

plus 1 for the topping

1 teaspoon olive oil

Juice of ¼ lemon

Salt

Wash and dry the mushrooms, then cut them into ¼-inch (5-mm) slices. Put them into the steamer basket and pour water into the water reservoir to level 3. Cook for 15 minutes with a pinch of salt.

When cooked, add the hazelnuts, olive oil, and lemon juice and blend to a smooth puree. Grate the remaining hazelnut over the puree to add something chewable to the dish.

PREPARATION TIME
5 MINUTES
COOKING TIME
15 MINUTES

FROM
13
MONTHS

CAULIFLOWER POACHED IN MILK, RAS EL HANOUT

¼ cauliflower

⅓ cup plus 1½ tablespoons (100 ml) unsweetened growing-up milk

1 pinch ras el hanout

1 teaspoon olive oil

Cut off the cauliflower florets. Blanch the florets to make them more digestible: Put them into a saucepan of boiling water, cover, and heat for 1 to 2 minutes, then immediately immerse them in iced water to stop the cooking process.

Drain the cauliflower florets, then put them into the pasta/rice cooker with the milk and the ras el hanout. Fill the water reservoir to level 3 and cook for 15 minutes.

When cooked, blend with the olive oil to a smooth puree for younger children or mash with a fork for older ones.

PREPARATION TIME
5 MINUTES
COOKING TIME
15 MINUTES

FROM
13
MONTHS

SNOW PEAS
WITH OLIVES

2 handfuls snow peas
5 pitted black olives
1 teaspoon olive oil

Trim the snow peas, wash them under running wate,r then place in the put them into the steamer basket with the pitted black olives. Fill the water reservoir to level 3 and cook for 15 minutes.
When cooked, put the snow peas and olives into the blender and blend to a coarse consistency. Serve in a bowl, drizzled with a little olive oil.

PREPARATION TIME
10 MINUTES
COOKING TIME
15 MINUTES

FROM
13
MONTHS

RED SNAPPER SOUP

1 ounce (30 g) red snapper fillet
¼ fennel bulb
1 tomato
½ scallion
¼ clove garlic
1 teaspoon olive oil

Make sure that there are no bones in the red snapper fillet.

Wash the fennel and dry it. Remove the green fronds, cut out the heart, and finely slice the bulb. Wash the tomato. Remove the seeds from the tomato. Peel and finely chop the onion and garlic. Put everything into the steamer basket with the fish. Fill the water reservoir to level 3 and cook for 15 minutes. Set aside the cooking liquid.

When cooked, put everything into the blender, add the cooking liquid, and blend to a thin soup, adding a little water to loosen the mixture, if necessary.

Strain the soup through a conical strainer before serving and drizzle with a little olive oil.

THE NUTRITIONIST'S TIP

You can also serve this dish unblended so that your child can discover new textures and try eating small pieces of solid food.

THE SUN...

SUMMER

AND ALL OF
ITS DELIGHTS!

QUALITY:
THE BEST FOR MY BABY

It's perfectly normal that you demand the best for this wonderful baby that has just entered your lives! The best ingredients, produce, prepared foods, recipes. Nourish your baby well to be sure of good growth, that he or she will learn easily, that your child's body functions in the best way possible, that your child can bring out the best in him or herself, and that your baby discovers something essential: seasonal produce that tastes good. It is a responsibility, and so here is some help to make the right choices.

Ingredients

First, be sure to choose foods that are in season: fruit and vegetables that are flavorsome, that are fleshy and contain a lot of vitamins and minerals; good fish at the right time of year; meat from animals that are well fed so that their flesh and the products that come from them (eggs, dairy products, cheeses) are delicious, have texture, and are high in healthy nutrients.

Following the seasons—as we did for the recipes in this book—ensures your baby will have a naturally varied diet adapted to his or her specific needs all year round: citrus fruit in winter to boost his or her immune system; and tomatoes, melons, and watermelon in summer, whose high water content helps to hydrate on hot days.

You can also buy food that is grown in the most natural way possible by switching from conventional agriculture to favoring products that are, if not organic, at least from "responsible" or "sustainable" farming. For the latter, the use of chemicals (pesticides, insecticides, etc.) is limited and controlled, and the land is respected. This means that the final product is of good nutritional quality.

VEGETABLES

CARROTS, ZUCCHINI (SEEDED),
FENNEL, GREEN BEANS
(EXTRA—SMALL), LAITUE,
SWEET POTATO,
SALAD GREENS

FRUITS

APRICOT, BANANA,
MIRABELLE, NECTARINE,
PEACH, PRUNE

Of course, organic, if it is seasonal and local, is good for one's diet in general and that of babies in particular. Because preparing meals for children requires small amounts of ingredients, it is something within reach of all budgets.

Containers

Containers are linked to the quality of your child's meals, both those in which you prepare the meals and those from which your baby eats. To keep your baby as healthy as possible, Béaba® has designed Babycook Néo® with the most neutral materials available—no plastic comes into contact with the food.

In the same way, the skillets and saucepans that are used to prepare meals, the plates in which they are served, the flatware with which they are eaten, etc., are best if made from materials such as cast iron, glass, metal, ceramic, porcelain. Of course, they are more fragile than plastic, but they are more neutral. And if it is difficult to do without plastic, which is found everywhere, over time and whenever possible try to choose glass containers, because they are safer when it comes to transmitting nanoparticles to food.

Food preparation

Finally, the way you prepare food will also ensure optimum, quality meals.

The gentle steaming of food, the healthiest way of cooking that we know of, guarantees that most vitamins and minerals are not lost. Blending, for a more or less smooth result, gives you the possibility of meeting the needs of your baby according to his or her age and ability to eat specific textures.

Because of a demand for quality at each stage when preparing meals, your baby is fed a diet that is nutritionally more efficient, more flavorsome, and more adapted to his or her needs.

PREPARATION TIME
10 MINUTES
COOKING TIME
10 MINUTES

FROM
4 TO 6
MONTHS

ZUCCHINI IN RICE PAPER WRAPPERS

1 yellow zucchini
2 rice paper wrappers

Wash the zucchini, then cut it into 3½-inch (9-cm) sticks. Soak the rice paper wrappers in water for a few seconds to soften them, then wrap each zucchini stick in rice paper.

Place the zucchini rolls in the steamer basket, fill the water reservoir to level 2, and cook for 10 minutes.

For young babies, blend to a smooth puree.

From 10 months, your baby can nibble on the zucchini stick wrapped in rice paper.

THE NUTRITIONIST'S TIP

Start by seeing if your baby can eat zucchini on its own. If your baby likes it, you can move on to this more complete recipe.

PREPARATION TIME
10 MINUTES
COOKING TIME
10 MINUTES

GREEN BEANS, PEACH

1 handful fresh, young green beans
1 white peach
1 teaspoon olive oil (from 7 to 8 months)

Trim the green beans, wash them, and drain. Peel the peach, remove the pit, and cut the flesh into small dice. Put the green beans and peach into the steamer basket, fill the water reservoir to level 2, and cook for 10 minutes.

When cooked, put the green beans and peach into the blender and blend to a smooth consistency.

For older babies, from 9 months:
Peel the peach and cut it into ⅛-inch (3-mm) dice. When the greens beans are cooked, put them into the blender with the olive oil and blend to a smooth puree.

Sprinkle the diced peach over the beans and drizzle with 1 teaspoon of olive oil.

THE NUTRITIONIST'S TIP

Before trying this recipe, make sure your baby can digest both green beans and peaches well on their own.

PREPARATION TIME
5 MINUTES
COOKING TIME
15 MINUTES

FROM
4 TO 6
MONTHS

APRICOT HALVES
WITH VERBENA

3 apricots
1 sprig verbena (or 4 dried leaves)
1 tablespoon chopped almonds

Wash and pit the apricots, then cut them into large pieces. Put into the steamer basket, fill the water reservoir to level 1, and cook for 5 minutes.

At the end of this first cooking, add the sprig of verbena in the seasoning diffuser ball. Fill the water reservoir to level 2 and cook for 10 minutes. Remove the seasoning diffuser ball then blend the apricots to a smooth soup.

For younger babies, from 9 months

Add the sprig of verbena in the steamer basket before the second cooking. When cooked, blend the apricots with the verbena leaves and chopped almonds to a smooth soup.

For older children, from 12 months

Wash the apricots and put them whole into the steamer basket, fill the water reservoir to level 1, and cook for 5 minutes.

Remove the apricots, cut in half, and remove the pits. Put the apricots back into the steamer basket with the sprig of verbena. Fill the water reservoir to level 2 and cook for 10 minutes.

When cooked, put the apricot halves on a little plate and sprinkle with the almonds; make sure these are finely chopped to avoid them going down the wrong way.

PREPARATION TIME
5 MINUTES
COOKING TIME
15 MINUTES

FROM
7 TO 8
MONTHS

GRATED ZUCCHINI, COD, PARMESAN CHEESE

½ zucchini

⅜ ounce (10 g) cod fillet

1 teaspoon olive oil

1 tablespoon grated Parmesan
cheese (from 9 months)

Wash the zucchini under running water and grate it with a cheese grater. Put the grated zucchini into the pasta/rice cooker, place the cod on top, then fill the water reservoir to level 3. Cook for 15 minutes.
Up to 9 months: When cooked, put everything into the blender and blend with the olive oil to a smooth puree.

For older children, from 9 months: Place the cooked food on a plate, break up the cod into small pieces, and serve with a little grated Parmesan cheese.

PREPARATION TIME
10 MINUTES
COOKING TIME
5 MINUTES

FROM
7 TO 8
MONTHS

ZUCCHINI, MINT, AND RICOTTA

1 zucchini
1 tablespoon ricotta
4 mint leaves

Wash and dry the zucchini, then cut it into ¼-inch (5-mm) dice. Wash and dry the mint leaves. Put the zucchini into the steamer basket with the mint, fill the water reservoir to level 1, then cook for 5 minutes without adding salt.

When cooked, add the ricotta and blend the mixture to a smooth puree.

THE CHEF'S TIP

Because ricotta already contains enough salt, there's no need to add it.

PREPARATION TIME
10 MINUTES
COOKING TIME
10 MINUTES

FROM
7 TO 8
MONTHS

FENNEL AND POLLACK

½ fennel bulb

⅜ ounce (10 g) pollack fillet

1 teaspoon olive oil

A few drops of lemon juice

Wash the fennel and finely slice it by removing the green fronds, cutting out the heart, and cutting the bulb into thin strips. Fill the water reservoir to level 2. Put half of the fennel into the steamer basket, add the pollack, and then the remaining fennel. Cook everything for 10 minutes.

Put the cooked ingredients into the blender with the olive oil and lemon juice, then blend to a smooth puree.

PREPARATION TIME
10 MINUTES
COOKING TIME
10 MINUTES

FROM
7 TO 8
MONTHS

PEAS, MINT, DUCK

3 handfuls fresh, baby peas
4 mint leaves
⅜ ounce (10 g) fresh duck breast slices
1 teaspoon olive oil

Shell the peas and put them into the pasta/rice cooker with the mint and duck. Fill the water reservoir to level 2 and cook for 10 minutes.

When cooked, set aside the cooking liquid. Put the minted peas and duck into the blender and blend to a smooth puree with the olive oil, adding the cooking liquid, if needed.

For older babies, from 9 months and up, you can also set aside some of the duck breast, finely chop it, and sprinkle it over the puree.

PREPARATION TIME
10 MINUTES
COOKING TIME
10 MINUTES

FROM
9 TO 12
MONTHS

SWISS CHARD AND BABY PEAS

2 handfuls baby peas
1 Swiss chard, stem removed
½ scallion
1 pinch grated horseradish (from 18 months)
1 teaspoon olive oil

Shell the baby peas. Wash the Swiss chard leaf and scallion under running water, then slice into ¼-inch (5-mm)-long strips.

Mix all the vegetables in the steamer basket and pour water into the water reservoir to level 2. Cook for 10 minutes.

Depending on your baby's development, you can either blend everything with the olive oil to a thick puree or mash the vegetables with a fork and drizzle with the olive oil.

From 18 months, season with a little grated horseradish.

THE CHEF'S TIP

If your baby does not finish all of the puree, you can store it in the refrigerator until the next day.

PREPARATION TIME
10 MINUTES

COOKING TIME
10 MINUTES

FROM
9 TO 12
MONTHS

CAPONATA

½ zucchini
½ eggplant
1 tomato
6 arugula leaves
1 teaspoon olive oil
1 garlic clove (from 12 months)

Wash the zucchini, eggplant, and tomato under running water. Peel and seed the tomato.

Cut all the vegetables into ⅜-inch (1-cm) dice. Put them into the steamer basket, fill the water reservoir to level 2, and cook for 10 minutes.

Wash and dry the arugula.

When cooked, coarsely blend the vegetables with the arugula leaves and olive oil, depending on your baby's development.

THE CHEF'S TIP

If you want, cook one garlic clove in the seasoning diffuser ball with the vegetables to enhance the flavor of the caponata, but remember to remove it before blending. If you would like to add the garlic to the dish itself, do so only when your baby is 12 months old.

MELON
AND GOAT'S CHEESE

¼ ripe melon

1 mint leaf

Juice of ¼ lemon

2 tablespoons fresh goat cheese,
such as Petit Billy

Seed the melon and remove the rind. Cut the flesh into 1-cm dice. Put it into the blender with the mint and lemon juice, then blend to a soup.
Pour the soup into a bowl and sprinkle with the finely crumbled cheese.

For younger babies, from 7 to 8 months, put the melon, mint, and lemon into the steamer basket with the water reservoir filled to level 2. Cook for 10 minutes before blending with the cheese.

PREPARATION TIME
5 MINUTES
COOKING TIME
15 MINUTES

FROM
9 TO 12
MONTHS

APRICOT
AND PISTACHIO SOUP

3 apricots
½ lemon
2 glasses of water
1 tablespoon shelled pistachios

Wash the apricots and put them into the steamer basket with the water reservoir filled to level 1, then cook for 5 minutes. This will make it easier to peel them.

After the 5 minutes, remove the apricots from the steamer basket. Peel them, cut in half, and remove the pits. Put them back into the steamer basket, fill the water reservoir to level 2, and cook for another 10 minutes.

Put the apricot halves into the blender, squeeze the lemon juice over them, add the water, and blend to a soup. Serve in a bowl and sprinkle with the finely chopped pistachios.

STRAWBERRY AND WATERMELON FRAPPÉ

1 handful strawberries
1 small piece watermelon
½ lemon
4 ice cubes

Wash and hull the strawberries, cut in half, and put them into the blender. Remove the rind and seeds from the watermelon. Cut the flesh into large chunks and put into the blender.
Squeeze the lemon over the fruit, add the ice cubes, and, using the pulse button, blend to a cool and thick consistency.

PREPARATION TIME
10 MINUTES
COOKING TIME
10 MINUTES

FROM
9 TO 12
MONTHS

APPLE AND RHUBARB WITH VANILLA SUGAR

1 apple
1 stalk rhubarb
¼ vanilla bean, scraped

Peel the apple and stalk of rhubarb. Put the fruit into the steamer basket and fill the water reservoir to level 2. Cook for 10 minutes.

Drain the fruit and put them into the blender with the vanilla seeds. Blend to a smooth puree or mash with a fork, depending on your baby's development.

PREPARATION TIME
10 MINUTES
COOKING TIME
15 MINUTES

FROM
13
MONTHS

STEAMED EGGPLANT WITH CUMIN

1 eggplant
1 teaspoon cumin seeds
1 teaspoon white miso paste
1 teaspoon olive oil

Peel the eggplant and cut it into 2¾–3¼-inch (7–8-cm) sticks.

Finely chop the cumin seeds. Spread the eggplant sticks with the miso paste, then sprinkle with the chopped cumin and put it into the steamer basket. Fill the water reservoir to level 3 and cook the eggplant sticks for 10 minutes.

Depending on the development of your child, you can either blend everything to a thick puree in the blender or mash the eggplant with a fork, then drizzle with a little olive oil when ready to serve.

PREPARATION TIME
10 MINUTES
COOKING TIME
15 MINUTES

FROM
13
MONTHS

EGGPLANT BABAGANOUSH

1 eggplant
½ clove garlic
½ lemon
1 tablespoon tahini
Salt

Peel the eggplant and cut it into ⅜-inch (1-cm) dice. Peel and chop the garlic. Combine, add a tiny pinch of salt, and put into the steamer basket. Fill the water reservoir to level 3 and cook for 15 minutes.

Meanwhile, grate the zest of the lemon onto a plate, then squeeze it to extract the juice. Set aside.

When the eggplant is done, discard the cooking liquid. Put the cooked eggplant and garlic into the blender with the lemon juice and tahini. Blend just a little to mix all the ingredients. Sprinkle with the lemon zest.

PREPARATION TIME
5 MINUTES

COOKING TIME
15 MINUTES

FROM
13
MONTHS

ROMANESCO BROCCOLI, ALMONDS

½ romanesco broccoli
(or ¼ head each broccoli and cauliflower)
1 tablespoon shelled almonds
1 teaspoon olive oil

Wash the romanesco broccoli and cut off the florets. Put into the steamer basket and fill the water reservoir to level 3. Cook for 15 minutes.

When cooked, put the romanesco broccoli into the blender with the almonds and blend to a puree. The puree can be smooth or coarse, depending on your baby's development.

PREPARATION TIME
5 MINUTES
COOKING TIME
10 MINUTES

FROM
13
MONTHS

GREEN BEANS COOKED IN ALMOND MILK

1 small handful green beans

¼ cup (35 g) whole almonds

⅓ cup plus 1½ tablespoons (100 ml) almond milk

Trim the green beans and coarsely chop them.

Put the almonds, green beans, and almond milk into the pasta/rice cooker. Fill the water reservoir to level 2 and cook for 10 minutes.

When cooked, add the milk, almonds, and green beans to the blender, then blend to a smooth puree.

PREPARATION TIME
5 MINUTES
RESTING TIME
OVERNIGHT

FROM
13
MONTHS

CHERRY AND ALMOND MILK GRANITA

6 handfuls Burlat cherries
2 tablespoons almond milk
2 tablespoons growing-up milk

The previous day, wash, dry, and pit the cherries. Put two handfuls into the blender and blend until smooth. Strain the juice through a conical strainer and freeze the juice overnight.

The next day, put the remaining cherries into the blender, pour in the almond milk and growing-up milk, and blend until smooth. Add a little water to the mixture if it is too thick, then strain through a conical strainer.

Remove the cherry granita from of the freezer and scrape it with a fork. Serve in a bowl over the cherry-milk mixture.

PREPARATION TIME
5 MINUTES
RESTING TIME
15 MIN

FROM
13
MONTHS

RASPBERRIES, CHIA

3 tablespoons raspberries

4 tablespoons coconut milk

6 tablespoons low-fat
or growing-up milk

¼ lime

2 tablespoons chia seeds

Wash the raspberries under running water and put them into the blender with the coconut milk and the low-fat or growing-up milk. Squeeze the lime over the contents of the blender and blend to a liquid. Put the chia seeds into a bowl and pour the raspberry mixture over them. Let stand for 15 minutes for the seeds to swell before serving.

PREPARATION TIME
10 MINUTES
RESTING TIME
OVERNIGHT

FROM
13
MONTHS

MELON-RASPBERRY ICE POPS

½ melon
½ lemon
125 g raspberries
1 tsp honey

The previous day, remove the rind from the melon, cut it into chunks, and put them into the blender. Squeeze the lemon juice over the melon, add the raspberries and honey, then blend to a liquid juice. Pour this mixture into four ice-pop molds or small coffee cups, then place an ice cream stick in each one. Let freeze overnight.
When about to serve, dip the molds or cups into a little hot water to unmold them more easily.

For younger babies, from 9 to 12 months, prepare these delicious ice pops without the honey.

WATERMELON AND STRAWBERRY MILK SHAKE, SCENTED WITH ORANGE FLOWER WATER

½ cup (75 g) watermelon (prepared)

75 g strawberries

2 to 4 drops of orange flower water

⅓ cup (80 g) growing-up milk

2 ice cubes

Peel and seed the watermelon, then cut into ¾-inch (2-cm) dice. Wash, hull, and halve the strawberries.

Put the fruit into the blender, add the orange flower water, milk, and ice cubes, and blend to a frothy liquid.

PREPARATION TIME
10 MINUTES
COOKING TIME
10 MINUTES

FROM
18
MONTHS

BABY FAVA BEANS WITH RICE MILK

3 handfuls baby fava beans
6 tablespoons rice milk

Shell the beans. Peel the larger ones but leave the skin on the smallest. Put the beans into the pasta/rice cooker and add the rice milk. Fill the water reservoir to level 2 and cook for 10 minutes.
When cooked, put everything into the blender and blend to a thick, coarse puree.

PREPARATION TIME
5 MINUTES
COOKING TIME
15 MINUTES

FROM
18
MONTHS

STEAMED MILLET, PORCINI, LINE-CAUGHT WHITING

1 ounce (30 g) whiting
3 pieces dried porcini
2½ tablespoons (30 g) millet
1 to 2 teaspoons olive oil

Remove the skin and bones from the whiting, then cut in half.

Chop the mushrooms with a knife and add to the millet. Put half of the mixture into the pasta/rice cooker, add the whiting, and top with the remaining millet-mushroom mixture. Fill the water reservoir to level 3 and cook for 15 minutes.

When cooked, put everything into the blender and blend to a smooth puree. Serve in a bowl, drizzled with a little olive oil.

THE CHEF'S TIP

For older babies, set aside a few pieces of fish and serve them, unblended, with the puree. The fish can also be crumbled over the puree so your baby has something to chew.

PREPARATION TIME
5 MINUTES
COOKING TIME
15 MINUTES

FROM
18
MONTHS

RESTING TIME
OVERNIGHT

CURRIED DUCK AND NAVY BEANS

1 ounce (30 g) chopped duck thigh
1 handful navy beans
½ teaspoon sweet curry powder
1 teaspoon duck fat

The previous day, put the navy beans into cold water to soak overnight.

The next day, drain the beans and put them with the curry powder and chopped duck into the pasta/rice cooker. Fill the water reservoir to level 3 and cook for 15 minutes.

When cooked, put the beans and duck into the blender and blend with the duck fat to a smooth puree, adding a little of the cooking liquid to loosen it, if necessary.

THE CHEF'S TIP

If your child accepts it, you don't have to puree the mixture; he or she should be able to eat the food as it is when it has finished cooking.

FALL

FALLING LEAVES...

AND HEARTY SOUPS!

THE SENSES:
ALL STIMULATED BY FOOD

When we think about food, we think mainly of the tastes we distinguish in our mouths. And yet, as your baby progresses along the journey of learning to eat solids, it means including and using all of his or her senses. In his recipes, Christophe Saintagne plays with textures and colors. During cooking, thanks to the cloud of steam that emerges from the Babycook®, the sense of smell is stimulated, as is the promise of a meal filled with emotions.

For the introduction of solid foods to be optimal—and for your baby to begin his or her taste repertoire—you will have to play with every one of the senses.

Starting with sight, early on, your baby sees the colors of what he or she eats, and this contributes to the pleasure that food offers. Your baby learns to associate colors with flavors: green for green beans, red for tomatoes, yellow for lemon. Later on, sight will be used to identify food that is perhaps damaged or not fit to eat. Thanks to his or her eyes, your baby also learns to understand different shapes. Growing up, your child will become aware of the way dishes are presented.

Surprisingly, hearing is extremely stimulated as you eat. Not only does it let us hear sounds related to food—the crunchiness of a baguette, the bubbles in sparkling water—but it contributes to the understanding of taste. It really does! Too overloaded in a noisy environment, the sense of hearing kicks into high gear and prevents you from properly understanding what you are eating. The best thing to do, therefore, for your baby's mealtimes, is to find a quiet environment without too much stimulation.

Eating is also about touching! Using his or her fingers, your baby feels the velvetiness of a peach's skin, the downy surface of a kiwifruit, or the sharp angles of a pineapple, but also your baby's tongue and mouth convey information whether something is hot, astringent, granular, stringy. Learning new words and sensations will be the result of all these experiences your baby feels.

BEFORE STARTING TO PREPARE CHRISTOPHE'S RECIPES, MAKE SURE YOUR BABY CAN DIGEST EACH OF THE INDIVIDUAL FOODS BELOW FROM WHEN HE OR SHE IS FOUR MONTHS OLD.

The sense of smell is directly related to taste—that's why everything seems bland when you have a blocked nose. Smelling an ingredient, a dish, is a good thing to teach your baby. Most important, so that your baby can rely on his or her sense of smell to distinguish between food that is fit to eat food and spoiled food. This sense also makes it possible to perceive aromas, those molecules that stimulate the nasal passages from the inside and that are released by food as soon as they are chewed.

But above all, smell is the promise of a flavor. Again, put into words what your baby is smelling: woody, floral, fruity smells, the smells of a childhood memory. All this is a great way to tell stories, remember, and share with your baby.

However, the peak of any sensory food experience is, of course, taste. Each baby has an incredible number of taste buds that send him or her a lot of information. Over the course of your child's life, some of these will be lost, and this may perhaps explain why a child's taste changes. It is also because we are all endowed with more or less sensitive taste buds, making it difficult to share the taste experience. One loves what another hates. Everyone has their reasons, and it's important to respect them without confining your child too quickly into a set pattern. Tomorrow your baby might love what he or she refused to eat yesterday.

VEGETABLES
RED BEET, LEEK (WHITE PART), BROCCOLI (FLORET), CARROTS, CITROUILLE, COURGE, FENNEL, PARSNIP, SWEET POTATO, PÂTISSON, POTIMARRON, PUMPKIN, SALAD GREENS

FRUITS
BANANA, QUINCE, PEAR, APPLE, RAISIN (SANS PEAU NI PÉPINS)

PREPARATION TIME
5 MINUTES
COOKING TIME
10 MINUTES

FROM
4 TO 6
MONTHS

STEAMED BROCCOLI, CRUNCHY STEM AND MINT

1 small head broccoli
1 drop vinegar
3 mint leaves
Salt (from 12 months)

For 4–6-month-old babies who have already eaten broccoli by itself and can assimilate it well.

Cut off the florets and wash them in the water and vinegar. Dry them and put into the steamer basket with the mint leaves. Fill the water reservoir to level 2. Cook for 10 minutes. You can also put the mint leaves in the seasoning diffuser ball to just aromatize the food.

When cooked, blend the broccoli florets and the mint leaves to a smooth puree.

From 9 months

After making the puree, peel the large broccoli stem and cut into ⅛-inch (3-mm) dice. Put into the steamer basket, fill the water reservoir to level 2, and cook for 10 minutes. Sprinkle the diced broccoli over the puree.

From 12 months

You can also add a little pinch of salt while cooking, and sprinkle the raw, diced broccoli over the puree.

FROM
4 TO 6
MONTHS

PREPARATION TIME
5 MINUTES
COOKING TIME
15 MINUTES

(GINGERY)
BUTTERNUT SQUASH

⅙ (150 g) butternut squash
(⅔ cup prepared)
⅜-inch (1-cm) piece ginger
(from 7 to 8 months)

From 4 months and up

Peel the butternut squash and cut it into ¾-inch (2-cm) dice. Place it in the steamer basket. Fill the water reservoir to level 3 and cook for 15 minutes. When cooked, blend the mixture to a smooth puree.

From 7 to 8 months

Peel the ginger, cut into dice, and put into the seasoning diffuser ball. Put the diced butternut squash and seasoning diffuser ball into the steamer basket. Fill the water reservoir to level 3 and cook for 15 minutes.

When cooked, remove the seasoning diffuser ball and blend the mixture to a smooth puree.

From 9 months

Finely grate the ginger over the butternut squash in the steamer basket. When cooked, put the mixture onto a plate and mash with a fork.

PREPARATION TIME
5 MINUTES
COOKING TIME
15 MINUTES

FROM
4 TO 6
MONTHS

STAR ANISE STEAMED QUINCE AND APPLE

½ quince

1 apple

½ lemon (from 7 to 8 months)

½ star anise

Peel the quince and apple, then cut them into ⅜-inch (1-cm) dice. Squeeze the lemon over the fruit to prevent it from changing color. Put the ingredients into the steamer basket with the star anise in the seasoning diffuser ball, fill the water reservoir to level 3, and cook for 15 minutes.

When cooked, remove the star anise, put the fruit into the blender, and blend to a smooth puree.

THE NUTRITIONIST'S TIP

Before mixing the ingredients, make sure that your baby can digest apples properly.

PREPARATION TIME
5 MINUTES

COOKING TIME
15 MINUTES

FROM
7 TO 8
MONTHS

WATERCRESS, ORGANIC SALMON

2 handfuls watercress

³⁄₈ oz (10 g) organic French salmon

Pluck the leaves from the watercress. Wash them in water with a little vinegar and dry them well. Put half of the leaves into the steamer basket, add the salmon, then add the remaining leaves. Fill the water reservoir to level 3 and cook for 15 minutes. Put the watercress and salmon into the blender. Do not discard the cooking liquid. Blend to a smooth puree, adding a little cooking liquid, if necessary.

NUTRITIONAL INFO

Because salmon is naturally oily, there's no need to add anymore fat.

PREPARATION TIME
5 MINUTES
COOKING TIME
25 MINUTES

FROM
7 TO 8
MONTHSS

YAM AND CHICKEN COLOMBO CURRY

1 slice (2¾ ounces/80 g) of yam
or sweet potato (½ cup prepared)
⅜ ounce (10 g) chicken breast
1 teaspoon olive oil
1 pinch Colombo spice blend

Peel the yam and cut into ⅜-inch (1-cm) dice. Put into the steamer basket with the spice blend, fill the water reservoir to level 3, and cook for 15 minutes. When cooked, fill the water reservoir again, this time to level 2, and add the chicken. Cook for another 10 minutes. Blend with the olive oil to a smooth puree and serve.

PREPARATION TIME
5 MINUTES

COOKING TIME
15 MINUTES

FROM
7 TO 8
MONTHS

RUTABAGA AND BEEF WITH TOMATO SAUCE

⅓ small rutabaga

1 potato

⅜ ounce (10 g) ground beef

1 tablespoon tomato sauce

1 teaspoon olive oil

Peel the rutabaga and potato, then cut them into ¼-inch (5-mm) dice. Put them into the steamer basket with the beef and tomato sauce.

Fill the water reservoir to level 3 and cook for 15 minutes.

When cooked, put the contents of the steamer basket in the blender and blend to a smooth puree with the olive oil.

PREPARATION TIME
5 MINUTES
COOKING TIME
15 MINUTES

FROM
9 TO 12
MONTHS

CREAMY BEET WITH WALNUTS

½ beet

4 walnuts

1 teaspoon olive oil

Salt (from 12 months)

Peel and thoroughly wash the beet under running water. Cut it into ¼-inch (5-mm) dice.

Fill the water reservoir to level 3 and cook for 15 minutes. Meanwhile, shell the walnuts and remove the kernels.

When cooked, put the beet into the blender, add the walnuts and oil, and blend until creamy in texture.

For older children, from 12 months, you can add a pinch of salt while cooking the beet. You can also finely grate 1 walnut and sprinkle it over the puree just before feeding it to your baby.

CAULIFLOWER, BROCCOLI, LEMON

¼ organic cauliflower
¼ organic broccoli
¼ organic lime
1 teaspoon olive oil

Wash the cauliflower and broccoli under running water, then cut off the florets. Put them into the steamer basket, fill the water reservoir to level 3, and cook for 15 minutes.

Put the vegetables into the blender, then grate the zest and juice the lemon into the blender jar. Blend with the olive oil to a smooth puree.

TOMATO, RED BELL PEPPER, TUNA

1 tomato
½ red bell pepper
1 basil leaf
½ glass of water
1 tablespoon tuna in oil
plus a few slivers to top
1 teaspoon oil from the can of tuna
¼ garlic clove (from 12 months)

Use a vegetable peeler to peel the tomato and the bell pepper. Remove the seeds and coarsely chop them.

Put them into the blender with the basil leaf, the water, tuna and oil. Blend to a soup and pour into a bowl. Finish by topping with the slivers of tuna.

From 12 months, you can add the peeled garlic to the blender to give the soup more flavor.

THE CHEF'S TIP

To make it easier to peel the tomatoes, immerse them for 10 seconds in boiling water.

PREPARATION TIME
5 MINUTES
COOKING TIME
15 MINUTES

FROM
9 TO 12
MONTHS

BASQUE-STYLE CHICKEN

¾ ounce (20 g) young chicken breast
from les Landes
¼ green bell pepper
¼ red bell pepper
1 scallion
½ clove garlic
½ tomato
1 teaspoon olive oil

Peel the bell peppers with a paring knife and remove the seeds. Peel the onion and garlic. Seed the tomato, then cut all the vegetables into ⅜-inch (1-cm) dice. Put the garlic into the seasoning diffuser ball and place it in the steamer basket with all the ingredients, including the chicken breast. Fill the water reservoir to level 3 and cook for 15 minutes. Set aside the cooking liquid.

When cooked, remove the seasoning diffuser ball and blend everything with the olive oil to a smooth puree, adding a little cooking liquid for younger babies or mashing everything with a fork if your baby is older.

THE NUTRITIONIST'S TIP

From 12 months, the garlic can be added to the steamer basket and blended with the vegetables.

BANANA
AND SORREL

1 banana
2 sorrel leaves
¼ lime

Wash the sorrel leaves under running water, then dry them well. Peel the banana and cut it into ⅜-inch (1-cm) slices.

Put the banana and sorrel into the blender jar, squeeze the lime and add the juice, then blend —without adding water—until it has a smooth texture. Serve cool.

For younger babies, put the sorrel leaves and banana into the steamer basket, fill the water reservoir to level 2, and cook for 10 minutes before blending.

THE NUTRITIONIST'S TIP

Prepare this recipe for your baby after it has already tried bananas and cooked sorrel.

PREPARATION TIME
5 MINUTES
COOKING TIME
15 MINUTES

FROM
9 TO 12
MONTHS

BEET
AND BLACKBERRIES

1 white beet (or red)
2 handfuls wild blackberries
A few drops of vinegar

Peel the beet and cut into ¼-inch (5-mm) dice. Wash the blackberries in water with a little vinegar. Put the diced beet into the steamer basket, fill the water reservoir to level 3, and cook for 15 minutes. When cooked, put the cooked beet into the blender, add the blackberries, and blend to a smooth puree.

THE CHEF'S TIP

From 9 months, add some finely chopped hazelnuts, which you can pick at the same time as the blackberries.

THE NUTRITIONIST'S TIP

If you want your baby to try this dish from 7 months, steam the blackberries with the beet.

PREPARATION TIME
10 MINUTES
COOKING TIME
15 MINUTES

FROM
13
MONTHS

ROSEMARY-SCENTED PORCINI BROTH

2 white mushrooms
⅛ ounce (4 g) dried porcini
4 rosemary leaves
1 to 2 teaspoons hazelnut oil

Stem the white mushrooms, wash the caps, and cut into ¼-inch (5-mm) dice. Chop the dried porcini and put them along with the mushrooms and rosemary into the steamer basket.

Fill the water reservoir to level 3 and cook for 15 minutes.

When cooked, put the cooking liquid, mushrooms, and rosemary into the blender. Blend with the oil, adding water if necessary, to obtain the desired consistency.

PREPARATION TIME
5 MINUTES
COOKING TIME
15 MINUTES

FROM
13
MONTHS

BUTTERNUT SQUASH AND WHITE MUSHROOMS

1½ cups (330 g) butternut squash
(prepared)
3 large, white mushrooms
2 teaspoons olive oil

Peel the squash and cut it into dice. Peel and wash the mushrooms, then cut two of them into quarters. Fill the water reservoir to level 3 and cook the mushroom quarters and squash into the steamer basket for 15 minutes. Set the cooking liquid aside. When cooked, put the cooked mushrooms and squash with the olive oil into the blender and blend with a little of cooking liquid to loosen the mixture. Serve the puree in a bowl and grate the remaining raw mushroom into fine flakes over it.

THE CHEF'S TIP

Any leftover puree can be frozen and served at another time.

Mushrooms are not easy to digest, so serve cooked mushrooms a few times to be sure your baby can assimilate them well before adding a raw mushroom to this recipe.

PREPARATION TIME
10 MINUTES
COOKING TIME
10 MINUTES

FROM
13
MONTHS

FIGS AND FENNEL

6 figs
¼ fennel bulb
2 tsp olive oil

Wash the figs and fennel under running water, then drain and dry.

Cut the fennel into ¼-inch (5-mm) dice, put into the steamer basket, then add the whole figs. Fill the water reservoir to level 3 and cook for 15 minutes.

When cooked, drain and put the contents into the blender. Blend with the olive oil to a smooth puree.

THE CHEF'S EXTRA TIPS

Because figs are naturally soft, you don't need to cut them up.

The aniseed flavor of fennel is a perfect counterbalance to the sweetness of the ripe figs.

PREPARATION TIME
5 MINUTES
COOKING TIME
15 MINUTES

FROM
13
MONTHS

CORN CAVIAR

2 (150 g) mini corn cobs
or 1 can organic corn kernels
1 teaspoon tahini
1 tsp olive oil

Use a knife to cut off the corn kernels and put them into the steamer basket with the water reservoir filled to level 3. Cook for 15 minutes.

When cooked, add the tahini, then blend to a coarse puree with the olive oil.

THE CHEF'S TIP

If you want, you can combine the cooked corn kernels with the tahini but not blend them.

TURNIPS, FIGS

3 turnips

½ teaspoon fennel seeds

1 fig

1 tbsp olive oil

Salt

Cut the greens off the turnips, peel with a knife, and coarsely chop. Finely chop the fennel seeds. Wash, dry, and coarsely chop the fig.

Put everything into the blender and blend to a smooth puree with the olive oil and a pinch of salt.

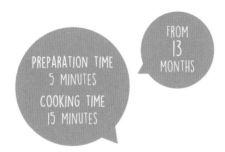

PREPARATION TIME
5 MINUTES
COOKING TIME
15 MINUTES

FROM
13
MONTHS

PARSNIPS, CHESTNUT HONEY

1½ parsnips
1 teaspoon chestnut honey
1 teaspoon olive oil

Wash the parsnips and cut into small dice. Fill the water reservoir to level 3 and cook for 15 minutes. Set aside the cooking liquid.

When cooked, put the parsnips into the blender and blend to a velvety consistency with the olive oil and a little of the cooking liquid.

Serve in a bowl drizzled with a little honey.

For younger babies, from 7 to 12 months, prepare the parsnip without the honey.

PREPARATION TIME
10 MINUTES
COOKING TIME
10 MINUTES

FROM
13
MONTHS

DAIKON RADISH, PEAR

⅓ daikon radish

1 pear, not too ripe

1 to 2 teaspoons olive olive oil

Peel the daikon and cut it into ⅛-inch (3-mm) dice. Peel the pear, cut it in half, and remove the seeds. Put everything into the steamer basket, fill the water reservoir to level 2, and cook for 10 minutes.

When cooked, remove the diced daikon. Put the pear into the blender and blend to a smooth puree. Mix the pear puree with the diced daikon in a small bowl and drizzle with a little olive oil.

PREPARATION TIME
5 MINUTES
COOKING TIME
10 MINUTES

FROM
13
MONTHS

CHOCOLATE PEAR

1 large cooking pear
¾ ounce (10 g) chocolate

Peel and core the pear, then cut the flesh into small dice. Put the dice into the steamer basket, fill the water reservoir to level 2, and cook for 10 minutes. Meanwhile, use a vegetable peeler to grate large flakes of chocolate.

When the pear is cooked, drain and blend it coarsely to a thick, lumpy coulis. Pour the coulis into a bowl and add the chocolate. Mix until it has melted well and serve.

CHESTNUTS, GREEN SALAD

4 lettuce leaves
1 drop vinegar
6 peeled chestnuts
2 teaspoons olive oil

Wash the lettuce leaves in the water and vinegar, then dry them well.

Put the chestnuts into the steamer basket, fill the water reservoir to level 3, and cook for 15 minutes. When cooked, put the chestnuts and cooking liquid into the blender and blend. Add the raw lettuce leaves and blend to a smooth puree.

CHICKPEA HUMMUS

3 tablespoons (30 g) cooked,
organic chickpeas
2 tsp tahini
1 teaspoon olive oil
Zest and juice of ½ lime

Put all the ingredients, except the lime zest, into the blender without any water. Blend to a smooth consistency.

Sprinkle with the lime zest and serve.

THE CHEF'S EXTRA TIPS

The protein in chickpeas is a great substitute for meat. To save time, used cooked, organic chickpeas; it would take too long to cook them in the Babycook®.

THE NUTRITIONIST'S TIP

Combine the protein of the chickpeas with those of a slice of bread for a perfect vegetarian meal.

PREPARATION TIME
5 MINUTES
COOKING TIME
15 MINUTES

FROM
24
MONTHS

SWEET POTATO, BLOOD SAUSAGE

1 ounce (30 g) boudin
du Béarn blood sausage
1 small sweet potato
1 pinch grated cardamom

Wash the sweet potato and cut into small dice. Cut the blood sausage into pieces.

Put everything into the steamer basket without adding any salt. Fill the water reservoir to level 3 and cook for 15 minutes.

When cooked, blend everything to a smooth consistency, or serve the blood sausage cut into little pieces and sprinkled over the puree.

THE CHEF'S TIP

Serve with steamed cauliflower or spinach for a truly well-balanced meal.

BRRR......

WINTER

WE NEED
WARMTH!

BETWEEN ANXIETY AND DISCOVERY: THE DIFFICULT JOB PARENTS HAVE IN NOURISHING THEIR CHILD

It is not easy for young parents to make the right choices in a food environment that has become stressful: the media, science, regulations, pesticides, insecticides, endocrine disruptors, child obesity, swallowing-related problems, etc. It's enough to make some parents break out in a cold sweat.

The food journey for feeding your child is made up of disconnected, slippery cobblestones. Food is integral. It means, therefore, becoming one with produce that is externally sourced. Depending on the way the produce was made or grown, on the transformations they have undergone, and on the personality of your child, a new family swings from discoveries, anxiety, and the joy of passing on what they know. A little advice and a few simple tips can really make life easier.

To the extent possible, try to put aside your worries about intensively farmed produce and the excessive use of pesticides and fertilizers. Organic, responsible, or sustainable farming are accessible alternatives. Moreover, local, seasonal produce is better for meeting your baby's needs and will be safer, too.

As for conservation and the transformation of produce, choose those that are more stable (in glass, ceramic, or stainless steel containers). Béaba® works with this in mind and is continually improving its Babycook® and its recipes in order to offer your baby the best possible quality.

To avoid too much contact with endocrine disruptors (molecules that interfere with the hormonal system), it is best to not use polycarbonate containers. They are indicated by the letters PC or the number 7 inside a triangle. This labeling is, unfortunately, not mandatory. Whenever possible, avoid heating food in or on plastic; instead, use glass, ceramic, or porcelain plates or stainless steel saucepans. Plastic has invaded our lives so much over recent years that it's hard to break the habit immediately. Think of it as a goal to achieve in the long term and keep it in mind.

And then there is your baby, this particular little eater whose moods change. Your baby eats at erratic times, has an appetite that seems huge to you, or, conversely, you don't know how to make him or her swallow a few mouthfuls. Your baby refuses the solid pieces but a cousin, who is the same age, might accept them.

You need to get to know this little eater, accept the way he or she is, as well as his or her personality, biorhythms, requirements, and skills that don't always happen when you expect them. The food journey must be taken step by step. Sometimes the pace is faster, sometimes it slows down. Don't worry about it. Don't make mealtimes a moment of conflict or for settling differences. Watch and observe your baby. Make sure he or she is on track on the growth chart and, if that is the case, everything is going well. The calmer you are, the better you can distance yourself from your baby's eating behavior without making it "your problem," and the better it will be over time, as well as being at the right pace.

VEGETABLES
LEEK (WHITE PART), BROCCOLI (FLORET), CARROTS, CITROUILLE, COURGE, FENNEL, PARSNIP, SWEET POTATO, PÂTISSON, POTIMARRON, PUMPKIN, SALAD GREENS

FRUITS
BANANA, PEAR, APPLE

FROM
7 to 8
MONTHS

PREPARATION TIME
5 MINUTES
COOKING TIME
15 MINUTES

CELERIAC, APPLE

½ celeriac (celery root)
1 apple
1 teaspoon lemon juice
1 teaspoon olive oil

Peel the celeriac and the apple and cut into dice. Fill the water reservoir to level 3, put all the ingredients into the steamer basket, and cook for 15 minutes. When cooked, blend the mixture into a smooth puree. Add the lemon juice and olive oil, and mix well.

From 9 months, you can cook the celeriac and then mash it with a fork. When the puree is ready, peel the apple, cut it into very small dice, and mix it in thoroughly with the lemon juice and olive oil.

PREPARATION TIME
10 MINUTES
COOKING TIME
10 MINUTES

FROM
7 TO 8
MONTHS

LEEKS, EGG, GARDEN HERBS

3 leeks
1 whole, organic egg
Fresh cilantro
Fresh parsley

Wash the leeks and remove the green part. Thickly slice the white part and put it into the steamer basket, making sure it does not overfill it.

Wash the egg's shell. Wash the herbs, then pluck off the leaves. Arrange the leeks around the sides of the basket and place the egg in the middle. Fill the water reservoir to level 2 and cook for 10 minutes.

Shell the egg, blend one-quarter of it with the leeks and herbs, adding a little of the cooking liquid to dilute the mixture.

For older babies, from 12 months

Cut the egg into little pieces and serve it on the side, or soft boil the egg and serve with strips of toast.

PREPARATION TIME
5 MINUTES
COOKING TIME
15 MINUTES

FROM
9 TO 12
MONTHS

CORNMEAL
AND CELERIAC

¼ head celeriac (celery root)

2 tablespoons (20 g) fine cornmeal
(corn flour)

1 saffron thread

1 teaspoon olive oil

Salt (from 12 months)

Peel the celeriac, cut it into small dice, and mix with the cornmeal. Put into the pasta/rice cooker and add the saffron thread. Fill the water reservoir to level 3 and cook for 15 minutes.

When cooked, put everything into the blender and blend with the olive oil to a smooth puree.

From 12 months, you can add a pinch of salt to the celeriac-cornmeal-saffron mixture.

159

PREPARATION TIME
5 MINUTES
COOKING TIME
20 MINUTES

FROM
9 TO 12
MONTHS

BASMATI RICE
WITH JERUSALEM ARTICHOKE

2 medium Jerusalem artichokes
4 teaspoons (15 g) basmati rice
1 teaspoon olive oil

Peel the Jerusalem artichokes, cut the flesh into small dice, and put them into the steamer basket. Fill the water reservoir to level 2 and cook for 10 minutes.

When cooked, transfer the Jerusalem artichokes to the pasta/rice cooker with the rice and cook for another 10 minutes with the water reservoir filled to level 2. Set aside some diced Jerusalem artichoke, then coarsely blend the rest with the olive oil and rice.

Sprinkle the diced Jerusalem artichoke over the puree.

THE CHEF'S TIP

Jerusalem artichokes are difficult to digest, and this is why I suggest you first cook them separately, before cooking them with the rice. They will be softer—thanks to being cooked twice—and will be much easier to digest.

PREPARATION TIME
5 MINUTES
COOKING TIME
15 MINUTES

FROM
9 TO 12
MONTHS

CARROTS, HONEY, GINGER

2 large carrots
1 pinch ground ginger
1 teaspoon honey (from 12 months)
1 drizzle olive oil

Peel and chop the carrots. Put the ginger in the seasoning diffuser ball. Fill the water reservoir to level 3 and cook everything for 15 minutes.

When cooked, removed the seasoning diffuser ball, put the carrots into the blender, add the honey and olive oil, and blend to a smooth puree.

For younger babies, from 7 to 8 months, prepare this dish without the honey or the oil.

For older children, from 12 months, you can add 1 teaspoon of honey to the blender with the carrots.

PREPARATION TIME
10 MINUTES
RESTING TIME
OVERNIGHT

FROM
9 TO 12
MONTHS

CLEMENTINE, GINGER GRANITA

6 to 8 organic clementines

⅜-inch (1-cm) piece ginger

The day before, rinse the clementines under running water. Peel the ginger.

Use a fine grater to zest the clementines and ginger onto a plate. Set aside.

Peel the clementines with a knife and remove the sections. Put into the blender, add the grated zest and ginger, and blend to a smooth puree. Pour into a deep plate and put into the freezer to harden overnight.

The next day, when it's your baby's mealtime, scrape the surface with a fork, put the granita into a small bowl, and serve immediately.

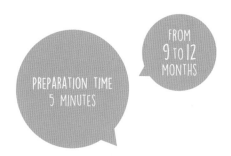

BANANA
AND KIWIFRUIT

½ banana

1 kiwifruit

¼ lime

Peel the banana and kiwifruit and cut into ⅜-inch (1-cm) slices.

Put the fruit into the blender jar, squeeze the lime and add the juice, then blend to a smooth puree.

167

PREPARATION TIME
5 MINUTES
COOKING TIME
15 MINUTES

FROM
9 TO 12
MONTHS

SEMOLINA WITH ORANGE ZEST

3 small handfuls fine semolina

1 orange

1 teaspoon olive oil

Finely grate the orange zest onto a small plate and set aside.

Place the semolina in the steamer basket and fill the water reservoir to level 3. Squeeze the orange and mix with the semolina. Cook everything for 15 minutes.

When cooked, put the semolina in a bowl, add the olive oil and sprinkle with the orange zest.

THE CHEF'S TIP

If you want your baby to try this dish from 7 months, cook the orange zest in the steamer basket with the semolina to make this flavor discovery, and digestion, easier.

PREPARATION TIME
5 MINUTES
COOKING TIME
15 MINUTES

FROM
13
MONTHS

CARROTS, CURRY, ORANGE

2 carrots

3 orange sections

Zest of ¼ orange

1 pinch curry powder

1 to 2 teaspoons olive oil

Peel and chop the carrots. Put them into the steamer basket and pour water into the water reservoir to level 3. Cook for 15 minutes with a pinch of salt. When cooked, put the carrots into the blender, add the orange sections, orange zest, and curry powder, and, using the pulse button, blend to a smooth puree.

From 9 months, you can make this dish but without any salt or olive oil.

PREPARATION TIME
5 MINUTES
COOKING TIME
15 MINUTES

FROM
13
MONTHS

CHICKEN, TURNIP, COCONUT, AND CURRY SOUP

2 turnips

1 ounce (30 g) chicken breast

½ teaspoon curry powder

2 tablespoons coconut milk

Peel and finely slice the turnips. Put them into the steamer basket with the chicken and curry powder. Fill the water reservoir to level 3 and cook for 15 minutes. Set aside the cooking liquid.

Put the curried turnips, chicken, and cooking liquid into the blender. Add the coconut milk and blend to a soup. Adjust the consistency by adding a little water, if necessary.

PREPARATION TIME
5 MINUTES
COOKING TIME
15 MINUTES

FROM
13
MONTHS

POTATO
AND OLIVE TAPENADE

1 new potato, such as Charlotte

½ clove garlic, skin on

1 teaspoon oil tapenade

Peel the potato, cut it into ⅜-inch (1-cm) dice, and put into the steamer basket with the ½ clove of garlic (left whole). Fill the water reservoir to level 3 and cook for 15 minutes.

When cooked, put the potato and peeled garlic into the blender and blend to a smooth puree.

Mix the tapenade into the potato puree and serve.

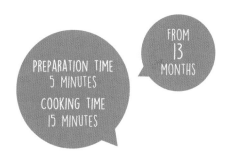

PREPARATION TIME
5 MINUTES
COOKING TIME
15 MINUTES

FROM
13
MONTHS

OYSTER MUSHROOMS AND ALMOND MILK

1 handful oyster mushrooms

¼ organic lemon

⅓ cup plus 1½ tablespoons (100 ml) almond milk

A few drops of vinegar

1 teaspoon olive oil

Salt

Cut the oyster mushrooms into 1½-inch (4-cm) pieces and carefully wash them in a bowl of water with a little vinegar. Drain and dry them, then put them into the steamer basket.

Squeeze the lemon over the oyster mushrooms and mix well. Add a pinch of salt and mix again. Fill the water reservoir to level 3 and cook for 15 minutes.

When cooked, pour the cooking liquid into the blender. Add the oyster mushrooms and almond milk, then blend to a smooth or coarse puree, depending on your baby's tastes.

PREPARATION TIME
5 MINUTES
COOKING TIME
10 MINUTES

FROM
13
MONTHS

TAPIOCA
AND COCONUT MILK

2 tablespoons (20 g) tapioca
2 tablespoons coconut milk
1 tablespoon low-fat or growing-up milk

Put the tapioca, coconut milk, and low-fat or growing-up milk into the pasta/rice cooker, fill the water reservoir to level 2, and cook for 10 minutes.

THE CHEF'S TIP

You can also aromatize the tapioca with some grated lime zest when it has finished cooking.

PREPARATION TIME
5 MINUTES

COOKING TIME
10 MINUTES

FROM
13
MONTHS

VICTORIA PINEAPPLE WITH COCONUT MILK

¾ cup (120 g) Victoria pineapple flesh (prepared)

2 tablespoons coconut milk

Cut the pineapple into ⅜-inch (1-cm) dice.

Put into the steamer basket, fill the water reservoir to level 2, and cook for 10 minutes.

When cooked, put the contents of the steamer basket into the blender, add the coconut milk, and blend to a thick puree. Serve cool.

THE NUTRITIONIST'S TIP

If you want to increase the amount of milk, add unsweetened growing-up milk to the coconut milk.

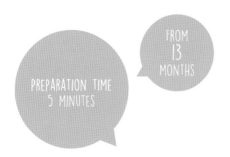

MANGO AND AVOCADO

 mango

½ avocado

¼ lemon

Peel the mango and remove the pit. Cut up the flesh and blend to a thick coulis.

Peel the avocado. Mash it with a fork to a smoother or coarser texture, depending on the age of your child. Squeeze the lemon and mix with the avocado. Serve the mango coulis and mashed avocado separately, or combine them for a mango-avocado puree.

PREPARATION TIME
10 MINUTES
COOKING TIME
10 MINUTES

FROM
18
MONTHS

SALSIFY
WITH FENNEL SEEDS

2 salsify roots

½ teaspoon fennel seeds

Peel the salsify roots, cut them into 4-inch (10-cm) pieces, and put them into the steamer basket.

Pound the fennel seeds in a mortar and add the salsify roots. Fill the water reservoir to level 2 and cook for 10 minutes.

When cooked, put everything into the blender and blend to a smooth consistency.

For a little more texture, blend to a coarse consistency.

PREPARATION TIME
5 MINUTES
COOKING TIME
15 MINUTES

FROM
24
MONTHS

KALE
WITH BACON

4 tender kales leaves

1 teaspoon diced bacon

Put the kale leaves and bacon into a saucepan. Cover with cold water and bring to a boil. When it reaches a boil, drain the leaves and bacon and put them into the steamer basket.

Fill the water reservoir to level 3 and cook for 15 minutes.

When cooked, blend the mixture to a smooth puree.

THE CHEF'S TIP

You can also set aside some of the cooked bacon, finely dice it, and mix into the puree.

PREPARATION TIME
5 MINUTES
COOKING TIME
15 MINUTES

FROM
24
MONTHS

ENDIVES, RAISINS, VIRE ANDOUILLE SAUSAGE

1 Belgian endive
3½ teaspoons (10 g) raisins
1 ounce (30 g) Vire andouille sausage
or other smoked sausage
1 tablespoon olive oil

Wash and finely chop the endive. Slice the Vire andouille sausage.

Put the endive into the steamer basket, then add the raisins and slices of sausage. Fill the water reservoir to level 3 and cook for 15 minutes.

When cooked, blend everything to a thick puree. For more texture and for your baby to experiment with more solid food, you can also prepare this without blending.

PREPARATION TIME
5 MINUTES

COOKING TIME
10 MINUTES

FROM
24
MONTHS

RED LENTILS
AND SMOKED BACON

2 handfuls red lentils
1 slice smoked bacon
5 parsley leaves

Put the red lentils and smoked bacon into the pasta/rice cooker. Fill the water reservoir to level 2 and cook for 10 minutes.

When cooked, put everything into the blender, add the parsley leaves, and blend to a smooth puree, adding a little water to loosen the mixture, if necessary.

THE CHEF'S TIP

If your baby accepts it, you can prepare this dish without blending it; serve the lentils when they are cooked and sprinkle the bacon, chopped into little pieces, over the top.

PREPARATION TIME
5 MINUTES

COOKING TIME
15 MINUTES

FROM
24
MONTHS

PUMPKIN AND RED ONION WITH BACON

1⅓ cups (150 g) pumpkin (prepared)

1 small red onion

2 slices smoked bacon

Peel the pumpkin and cut it into ⅜-inch (1-cm) dice. Peel the onion and chop finely.

Put the pumpkin and onion into the steamer basket and make a well in the middle. Place the bacon in the well. Fill the water reservoir to level 3 and cook for 15 minutes.

When cooked, blend with the olive oil to a smooth puree for younger babies or more coarsely for older ones.

THE CHEF'S TIP

Don't be afraid to give onions to young children; when onions are cooked, their sweetness is released.

APPENDICES

BY SEASON,
BY PRODUCT

AND BY
AGE !

TABLE OF CONTENTS

18 AWARENESS OF FLAVORS AND TEXTURES

20 Spinach, haddock

23 Spinach, egg and potatoes

25 Globe artichoke, arugula

26 Poivrade artichokes, lime

29 Cucumber, dill, and cream cheese

31 Parsley root, macaroni

32 Basil-scented bread and tomato soup

34 Mango and basil

37 Papaya and cream cheese soup

39 Green asparagus, tarragon

41 White mushrooms, hazelnuts

42 Cauliflower poached in milk, ras el hanout

44 Snow peas with olives

47 Red snapper soup

50 QUALITY: THE BEST FOR MY BABY

53 Zucchini in rice paper wrappers

54 Green beans, peach

57 Apricot halves with verbena

59 Grated zucchini, cod, parmesan cheese

60 Zucchini, mint, and ricotta

63 Fennel and pollack

64 Peas, mint, duck

66 Swiss chard and baby peas

69 Caponata

70 Melon and goat's cheese

72 Apricot and pistachio soup

74 Strawberry and watermelon frappé

77 Apple and rhubarb with vanilla sugar

79 Steamed eggplant with cumin

80 Eggplant babaganoush

82 Romanesco broccoli, almonds

84 Green beans cooked in almond milk

87 Cherry and almond milk granita

88 Raspberries, chia

91 Melon-raspberry ice pops

93 Watermelon and strawberry milk shake, scented with orange flower water

94 Baby fava beans with rice milk

97 Steamed millet, porcini, line-caught whiting

98 Curried duck and navy beans

FALL

102 THE SENSES: ALL STIMULATED BY FOOD

105 Steamed broccoli, crunchy stem and mint

106 (Gingery) butternut squash

109 Star anise steamed quince and apple

111 Watercress, organic salmon

112 Yam and chicken Colombo curry

114 Rutabaga and beef with tomato sauce

116 Creamy beet with walnuts

119 Cauliflower, broccoli, lemon

121 Tomato, red bell pepper, tuna

122 Basque-style chicken

125 Banana and sorrel

127 Beet and blackberries

128 Rosemary-scented porcini broth

131 Butternut squash and white mushrooms

133 Figs and fennel

135 Corn caviar

136 Turnips, figs

WINTER

139 Parsnips, chestnut honey

140 Daikon radish, pear

143 Chocolate pear

145 Chestnuts, green salad

147 Chickpea hummus

148 Sweet potato, blood sausage

152 BETWEEN ANXIETY AND DISCOVERY: THE DIFFICULT
JOB PARENTS HAVE IN NOURISHING THEIR CHILD

154 Celeriac, apple

157 Leeks, egg, garden herbs

159 Cornmeal and celeriac

160 Basmati rice with Jerusalem artichoke

162 Carrots, honey, ginger

164 Clementine, ginger granita

167 Banana and kiwifruit

169 Semolina with orange zest

170 Carrots, curry, orange

172 Chicken, turnip, coconut, and curry soup

174 Potato and olive tapenade

177 Oyster mushrooms and almond milk

178 Tapioca and coconut milk

181 Victoria pineapple with coconut milk

183 Mango and avocado

185 Salsify with fennel seeds

187 Kale with bacon

189 Endives, raisins, Vire andouille sausage

191 Red lentils and smoked bacon

192 Pumpkin and red onion with bacon

INDEX BY AGES

4 TO 6 MONTHS

MAIN DISHES

106 (Gingery) butternut squash
VARIATIONS FOR 7 TO 8 MONTHS — 9 MONTHS

54 Green beans, peach
VARIATIONS FOR 7 TO 8 MONTHS — 9 MONTHS

105 Steamed broccoli, crunchy stem and mint
VARIATIONS FOR 9 MONTHS — 12 MONTHS

53 Zucchini in rice paper wrappers
VARIATION FOR 10 MONTHS

SWEET

57 Apricot halves with verbena
VARIATION FOR 7 TO 8 MONTHS

109 Star anise steamed quince and apple
VARIATIONS FOR 9 MONTHS — 12 MONTHS

7 TO 8 MONTHS

MAIN DISHES

154 Celeriac, apple

63 Fennel and pollack

59 Grated zucchini, cod, parmesan cheese
VARIATION FOR 9 MONTHS

157 Leeks, egg, garden herbs
VARIATION FOR 12 MONTHS

64 Peas, mint, duck
VARIATION FOR 9 MONTHS

114 Rutabaga and beef with tomato sauce

20 Spinach, haddock
VARIATION FOR 9 MONTHS

23 Spinach, egg and potatoes
VARIATION FOR 12 MONTHS

111 Watercress, organic salmon

112 Yam and chicken Colombo curry

60 Zucchini, mint, and ricotta

9 TO 12 MONTHS

MAIN DISHES

32 Basil-scented bread and tomato soup

160 Basmati rice with Jerusalem artichoke

122 Basque-style chicken

69 Caponata
VARIATION FOR 12 MONTHS

162 Carrots, honey, ginger
VARIATIONS FOR 7 TO 8 MONTHS — FOR 12 MONTHS

119 Cauliflower, broccoli, lemon

159 Cornmeal and celeriac
VARIATION FOR 12 MONTHS

116 Creamy beet with walnuts
VARIATION FOR 12 MONTHS

29 Cucumber, dill, and cream cheese
VARIATION FOR 7 TO 8 MONTHS

25 Globe artichoke, arugula
VARIATION FOR 12 MONTHS

70 Melon and goat's cheese
VARIATION FOR 7 TO 8 MONTHS

26 Poivrade artichokes, lime
VARIATION FOR 12 MONTHS

37 Papaya and cream cheese soup

31 Parsley root, macaroni

66 Swiss chard and baby peas
VARIATION FOR 18 MONTHS

121 Tomato, red bell pepper, tuna
VARIATION FOR 12 MONTHS

SWEET

77 Apple and rhubarb with vanilla sugar

72 Apricot and pistachio soup

127 Beet and blackberries
VARIATIONS FOR 7 MONTHS — 9 MONTHS

167 Banana and kiwifruit

125 Banana and sorrel

164 Clementine, ginger granita

34 Mango and basil
VARIATION FOR 7 TO 8 MONTHS

169 Semolina with orange zest
VARIATION FOR 7 MONTHS

74 Strawberry and watermelon frappé

FROM 13 MONTHS

MAIN DISHES

131 Butternut squash and white mushrooms

170 Carrots, curry, orange
VARIATION FOR 9 MONTHS

42 Cauliflower poached in milk, ras el hanout
VARIATION DEPENDING ON YOUR BABY'S DEVELOPMENT

172 Chicken, turnip, coconut, and curry soup

135 Corn caviar

140 Daikon radish, pear

80 Eggplant babaganoush

133 Figs and fennel

39 Green asparagus, tarragon

84 Green beans cooked in almond milk

177 Oyster mushrooms and almond milk

139 Parsnips, chestnut honey
VARIATION FOR 7 TO 8 MONTHS

174 Potato and olive tapenade

47 Red snapper soup

82 Romanesco broccoli, almonds

128 Rosemary-scented porcini broth

44 Snow peas with olives

79 Steamed eggplant with cumin
VARIATION DEPENDING ON YOUR BABY'S DEVELOPMENT

136 Turnips, figs

41 White mushrooms, hazelnuts

SWEET

87 Cherry and almond milk granita

143 Chocolate pear

183 Mango and avocado

91 Melon-raspberry ice pops
VARIATION FOR 9 MONTHS

88 Raspberries, chia

178 Tapioca and coconut milk

181 Victoria pineapple with coconut milk

93 Watermelon and strawberry milk shake,
scented with orange flower water

MAIN DISHES

FROM
18
MONTHS

94 Baby fava beans with rice milk

145 Chestnuts, green salad

147 Chickpea hummus

98 Curried duck and navy beans

185 Salsify with fennel seeds

97 Steamed millet, porcini, line-caught whiting
VARIATION FOR 24 MONTHS

FROM
24
MONTHS

189 Endives, raisins, Vire andouille sausage

187 Kale with bacon

192 Pumpkin and red onion with bacon

191 Red lentils and smoked bacon

148 Sweet potato, blood sausage

INDEX BY PRODUCTS

SPRING

Asparagus 39
Cauliflower 42, 119
Cucumber 29
Dill 29
Globe artichoke 25
Haddock 20
Hazelnuts 40
Papaya 37
Parsley 157, 190
Poivrade artichoke 26
Spinach 20, 23
Tarragon 39
White mushrooms 40, 128, 131

SUMMER

Almonds 57, 82, 84
Apple 77, 109, 154
Apricot 57, 72
Beans (dried) 98
Cherries (Burlat) 87
Chia seeds 88
Eggplant (aubergine)
  69, 79, 80
Fava beans (baby)
  (broad beans) 94
Fennel 47, 63

Fennel bulb 133
Goat cheese 70
Green beans 54, 84
Hake 97
Melon 70, 91
Millet 97
Mint 60, 64, 70, 105
Olives (black) 44
Orange flower water 93
Peas 64, 66
Pollack 63
Porcini 97, 128
Raspberries 88, 91
Rhubarb 77
Red snapper 47
Romanesco broccoli 82
Scallion 32, 47, 66, 122
Snow peas (mange tout) 44
Strawberries 74, 93
Swiss chard 66
Tomato 32, 47, 69, 121, 122
Watermelon 74, 93
White peach 54
Zucchini (courgette)
  59, 60, 69
Zucchini (courgette)
  (yellow) 53

FALL

Banana 125, 167
Beet (beetroot) 116
Beet (white) 127
Bell pepper (green) 122
Bell pepper (red) 121, 122
Blackberries (wild) 124
Broccoli 105, 119
Butternut squash 106, 131
Chestnuts 145
Chicken (young) 122
Corn (sweetcorn) 135
Daikon 140
Fennel (seeds) 136, 185
Fig 133, 136
Ginger 106, 162, 164
Pear 140, 143
Quince 109
Rutabaga (swede) 114
Salad greens 145
Salmon 111
Sorrel 125
Star anise 109
Sweet potato 112, 148
Turnip 136, 172
Walnuts 116
Watercress 111
Yam 112

WINTER

Andouille sausage 189
Avocado 183
Carrot 162, 170
Celeriac (celery root) 154, 159
Clementine 164
Endive 189
Kale 187
Kiwifruit 167
Jerusalem artichoke 160
Leek 157
Onion, red 192
Orange 169, 170
Orange (zest) 170
Oyster mushroom 177
Pineapple 181
Pumpkin 192
Raisins 189
Salsify 185

ALL YEAR ROUND

Almond milk 84, 87, 177
Arugula (rocket) 25, 69
Bacon 187
Bacon (smoked) 190, 192
Basil 32, 34, 121

Beef 114
Blood sausage 148
Bread (crust) 32
Cardamom 148
Chestnut honey 139
Chicken 112, 172
Chickpeas 147
Chocolate 143
Cilantro (coriander) 157
Colombo curry mix 112
Coconut milk 88, 172, 178, 181
Cod 59
Cornmeal
Cream cheese 29, 37
Cumin 79
Curry 98, 170, 172
Duck 64, 98
Eggs 23, 157
Garlic (clove) 32, 47, 69, 80, 121, 122, 174
Growing up milk 42, 87, 88, 93, 178
Hazelnut oil 128
Honey 91, 162
Horseradish 66
Lemon 25, 39, 40, 63, 70, 72, 74, 80, 91, 109, 154, 177, 183
Lentils (red) 190

Lime 26, 88, 119, 125, 147, 167
Macaroni 31
Mango 34, 183
Olive tapenade 174
Parmesan cheese 59
Parsnip 31, 139
Pistachios 72
Cornmeal 159
Potato 23, 114, 174
Ras el hanout 42
Rice, basmati 160
Rice milk 94
Rice paper wrappers 53
Ricotta cheese 60
Rosemary 128
Saffron (threads) 159
Semolina (fine) 169
Semi-skimmed milk 88, 178
Tahini 80, 135, 147
Tapioca 178
Tuna (canned) 121
Tomato (sauce) 114
Vanilla bean 77
Verbena 57
Vinegar 105, 127, 145, 177
White miso 79

203

ACKNOWLEDGMENTS

CHRISTOPHE SAINTAGNE AND LAURA PORTELLI

Thank you to Anthony Denon-Madinska for
the wonderful, quality work he has done for this book.
And above all, thank you to our two children, Paul
and Émile, who inspire us every day.

LAURENCE HAURAT

Thank you to my mother and grandmothers,
two generations of women who introduced
everyday cooking to my lively taste buds right
in front of my amazed eyes. They have given me
a taste for good things.
Thank you to Fred, my own personal chef,
who wonderfully transforms day-to-day cooking
and who, with Marius, makes every day more
beautiful.
And thank you, also, to Claire Rebussi, my little
angel from the East.

BÉABA

A huge thank you to Laurence, Laura,
and Christophe, who have poured so much
passion and generosity into this book, which
is aimed at all young parents who, every day
and every moment, seek to offer the very best
to their children.

Thank you also to Fanny and Aurore for having
perfectly undertaken this beautiful book through
to the end.

COLLECTION DIRECTOR
Alain Ducasse

DIRECTOR
Aurore Charoy

EDITOR
Fanny Morgensztern

PHOTOGRAPHY
© Virginie Garnier

FOOD STYLING
Coralie Ferreira

ART DIRECTION AND GRAPHIC DESIGN
Soins Graphiques
Pierre Tachon, Camille Demaimay, and Aurélie Mansion

PHOTOENGRAVING
Nord Compo

Printed in China by Toppan.

ISBN: 978-2-37945-004-4
Legal deposit 4th quarter 2018